SAINT CATHERINE OF SIENA

&

SAINT PADRE PIO

PARACLETE PRESS

BREWSTER, MASSACHUSETTS

2019 First Printing

Set the World on Fire

Copyright © 2019 by Paraclete Press, Inc.

ISBN 978-1-64060-227-4

The Paraclete Press name and logo (dove on cross) are trademarks of Paraclete Press, Inc.

Library of Congress Cataloging-in-Publication Data is available.

10 9 8 7 6 5 4 3 2 1

All rights reserved. No portion of this book may be reproduced, stored in an electronic retrieval system, or transmitted in any form or by any means—electronic, mechanical, photocopy, recording, or any other—except for brief quotations in printed reviews, without the prior permission of the publisher.

Published by Paraclete Press
Brewster, Massachusetts
www.paracletepress.com

Printed in Canada

SAINT CATHERINE OF SIENA

SAINT CATHERINE OF SIENA

1

"Be who God meant you to be and you will set the world on fire."

2

"Proclaim the truth and do not be silent through fear."

3

"We've had enough exhortations to be silent. Cry out with a thousand tongues. I see the world is rotten because of silence."

4

"The soul is in God and God in the soul, just as the fish is in the sea and the sea in the fish."

Saint Catherine of Siena

5

"Pride displeases God. Humility pleases Him. In fact, so greatly did the virtue of humility please God in Mary that He was convinced to give her the Word, His only begotten Son. This is how she then became the sweet mother who gave Him to us."

6

"There is no obedience without humility,
or humility without love. This is shown
to us by the Word Himself, for in
obedience to His Father and in humility,
Christ ran to the shameful death
of the Cross."

7

"Nails were not enough to hold the God-
Man nailed and fastened on the Cross.
Love held Him there."

Saint Catherine of Siena

8

"Sometimes when it seems that God has taken much away from you, nearly every tie that binds you to the world, it is because He is calling you to great perfection."

9

"Now then, I want you to completely destroy your own will, so that it will cling to nothing but Christ crucified. In this way, you will fulfill His will and my desire for you."

10

"I will say no more. Remain in the holy and sweet grace of God. Sweet Jesus, Jesus Love."

Set the World on Fire

11

"Our heart ought to be made like a lamp, for just as a lamp is wide on top and narrow below, so the heart is. We ought always to keep it wide above, through holy thoughts, holy imaginations, and continual prayer."

12

"I said that a lamp is narrow below, and so is our heart, in order to signify that the heart ought to be narrow toward earthly things. It must not desire or love them extravagantly, or hunger for more than God wills to give us. Our hearts should always thank Him, seeing how sweetly He provides for us so that we never lack anything."

Saint Catherine of Siena

13

"Our heart will be a lamp only if there is enough oil within. This oil is that sweet little virtue, profound humility. And we cannot attain this virtue without true knowledge of ourselves—knowing our misery and frailty, that by ourselves can do no good deed, or escape any conflict or pain. . . . Abide in the knowledge of the goodness of God."

14

"God has created us in His image and likeness, and re-created us in grace by the blood of His only-begotten Son, the sweet incarnate Lord. Reflect on how continually the goodness of God works in us."

Set the World on Fire

15

"Sometimes we want to see all the servants of God walking in the same way that we are walking in ourselves. For example, it frequently happens that a soul which sees itself advancing by way of great penance wants to send all people by that same way, and if it sees that they do not walk there it is displeased and shocked, feeling that they're doing wrong. But it can happen that the person is doing better and being more virtuous than his critic, even though he does not do as much penance."

Saint Catherine of Siena

16

"Perfection does not consist in hurting the body, only in killing our perverse self-will. In this way, if the will is destroyed, we have submitted to the sweet will of God. Penance is good, but the rules are not the same for everyone."

17

"During the time ordained for prayer, the devil is apt to arrive in the soul, causing much more conflict and trouble than when the soul is not occupied in prayer. He does this so that holy prayer may become tedious to the soul. He tempts the soul often with these words: 'This prayer avails you nothing.'"

18

[God said to St. Catherine:] "The service you are unable to render to Me you must do for your neighbors. Thus, it will be evident that you have Me within your soul by grace."

19

"In your nature, eternal Godhead, I will come to know my nature. And what's my nature—boundless love? My nature is fire, because you are nothing but a Fire of Love, and you have given us a share in this nature, for by the Fire of Love you created us."

Saint Catherine of Siena

20

[God said to St. Catherine:] "The soul, as soon as she comes to know Me, reaches out to love her neighbors."

21

"Obedient people never trust in themselves."

22

"Hope comes from love, because people always trust in those they love."

23

"You, eternal Trinity, are a deep sea. The more I enter You, and the more I discover, the more I seek You."

24

"By the light of understanding within Your light, I have tasted and seen Your depth, Eternal Trinity, and the beauty of Your creation."

Saint Catherine of Siena

25

"You, Eternal Trinity, are the craftsman, and I Your handiwork have come to know that You are in love with the beauty of what You have made, since You made me a new creation in the blood of your Son."

26

"Holy Spirit, come into my heart. By Your power, draw my heart to you."

27

"It is only through shadows that one comes to know the light."

28

"To the servant of God every place is the right place, and every time is the right time."

29

"Every day you give yourself to us, representing yourself in the sacrament of the altar, in the body of your holy Church. What has done this? Your mercy. Oh, divine mercy! My heart suffocates in thinking of you, for everywhere I turn my thoughts, I find nothing but mercy."

Saint Catherine of Siena

30

"It is obedience which by the light of faith puts self-will to death. In a boat of obedience, a person will pass happily through the stormy seas of life, in peace of soul and tranquility of heart."

31

"Thanks, thanks be to you, supreme and eternal Father, satisfier of holy desires, and lover of our salvation, who, through your love, gave us Love Himself."

32

"O Supreme and Ineffable God, I have
sinned! Therefore, I am unworthy to
pray to You. But You can make me less
unworthy. Punish my sins, O Lord, but
do not turn away from my misery.
From You I have received a body which
I offer to You."

33

"O Mary, temple of the Trinity.
O Mary, bearer of fire.
O Mary, dispenser of mercy."

Saint Catherine of Siena

34

"O eternal Trinity, my sweet love!
You, light, give us light.
You, wisdom, give us wisdom.
You, supreme strength, strengthen us.
Today, Eternal God,
let our cloud be dissipated
so that we may perfectly know and
follow your Truth in truth,
with a free and simple heart.
God, come to our assistance!
Lord, make haste to help us!"

35

"Happiness cannot be found worthy to be compared with that of a soul in Purgatory, except that of the saints in Paradise. And day-by-day this happiness grows as God flows into these souls, as the hindrance to His entrance is consumed. The rust of sin is the hindrance, and the fire burns the rust away so that gradually the soul opens itself up to a divine inflowing."

36

"Penance should be but the means to increase virtue according to the needs of the individual, and according to what the soul sees she can do in the measure of her own possibility."

Saint Catherine of Siena

37

"You, O Mary,
are the new plant
from which we have the fragrant flower
of the Word,
only-begotten Son of God,
because this Word was sown in you,
O fruitful land.
You are the land and the plant.
O Mary, vehicle of fire,
you bore the fire hidden
and veiled beneath the ash of your
humanity."

38

"[God said to St. Catherine:] You need to see the gentle Loving Word born in a stable while Mary was on a journey—to show you pilgrims how you should be constantly reborn in the stable of self-knowledge, where by grace you will find Me born in your soul."

39

"You are rewarded not according to your work or your time but according to the measure of your love."

Saint Catherine of Siena

40

"[God said to St. Catherine:] The soul cannot live without love. She always wants to love something because love is the stuff she is made of, and through love I created her."

41

"When the soul is united with and transformed into Him, it is like fire consuming the dampness in logs. Once the logs are heated through and through, the fire burns and changes them into itself, giving them its own color and warmth and power."

Set the World on Fire

42

"[God said to St. Catherine:] You must walk my path on your two feet. You'll need two wings to fly to heaven."

43

"Prayer exercises the soul through humility and constancy, by uniting the soul to God as she follows the steps of Christ crucified."

Saint Catherine of Siena

44

"By desire and affection and union of love with Christ, the soul is transformed into Him. This seems to be what Christ meant when he said, 'They who have my commandments and keep them are those who love me; and those who love me will be loved by my Father, and I will love them and reveal myself to them' (Jn. 14:21)."

45

"Self-love is the sink-hole of every sin, and the root and cause of every evil."

46

"How could I be content, Lord, if any of those who have been created in Your image and likeness will perish? If your truth and justice permitted it, I would want Hell to be completely destroyed, or at least that no soul should ever again descend into it. If I were put over the mouth of Hell to close it, so that no one would ever again enter it, I would rejoice because all my neighbors would be saved."

Saint Catherine of Siena

47

"Lord, give me all the pains and infirmities that there are in the world, to bear in my body. I am ready to offer you my body in sacrifice."

48

"Great is the distance between what the intellect apprehends, rapt and illumined and strengthened by God, and what can be expressed with words."

49

"Don't you see?—I am no longer who I was. I am changed into another person!"

50

[St. Catherine wrote to the Pope:] "I ask you to follow Christ's footsteps with a courageous heart and evident zeal, never turning aside because of pain or pleasure, but persevering to the end in everything you do for Christ crucified."

Saint Catherine of Siena

51

[St. Catherine wrote to the Pope:] "Most holy Father, God has set you as shepherd over his little sheep . . . in a time when sin abounds in your subjects, in the body of holy Church, and throughout all Christendom, more than it has done for ages. It is for this reason, all the more, that you need be rooted in love, with pearls of justice."

52

"Today I want to begin anew, so that my sins may not hold me back from the great joy of giving my life for Christ."

53

"My soul feels more happiness
than I can say."

54

"If I were to give my body to be burned,
it doesn't seem to me that I could
possibly be giving back to Him nearly as
much as the grace
I have already received."

55

"Tell him to have pity and compassion on
those souls who are in great darkness."

Saint Catherine of Siena

56

"Throw the hatred in your hearts, and your self-love, on the ground, if you ever want to reform your city."

57

"We are in God's hands, either for justice or for mercy. It is better for us to acknowledge our faults and abide in the hands of mercy than to remain in sin—for our faults will not go unpunished."

58

"I will pledge myself to bear you up in the sight of God, with tears and continual prayers, and to bear the penance together with you, if you will please return to the Father."

59

"Pray and ask others to pray to God and to Mary, so that God may equip us to do what honors Him."

60

"I don't want you to look back for anything. Glory in your adversity. It is by enduring that we show our love and faithfulness, and give glory to God's name."

Saint Catherine of Siena

SAINT CATHERINE OF SIENA was born Caterina di Giacomo di Benincasa on March 25, 1347, in Siena, Italy, during an outbreak of plague. She was born a twin, but her sister did not survive. She began having visions of Christ while a young girl. At sixteen, Catherine was asked to marry the widower left behind when one of her older sisters died in childbirth. She refused, and in protest she began to fast, and she cut her hair. Soon she became a member of the Third Order of St. Dominic.

At the age of twenty-one, St. Catherine experienced what she described to Blessed Raymond of Capua, O.P., her spiritual director, as a "mystical marriage" to Christ. She also heard from Christ a directive to become more involved in the world. Soon, she was involved in politics and Church affairs, carrying on an extensive correspondence with fellow religious, bishops, cardinals, and popes. She was known, too, for rebuking the leaders of her Church when God instructed her to do so. God's messages to St. Catherine are recorded in her Dialogues.

St. Catherine died in 1380 in Rome at the age of thirty-three. She was canonized on June 29, 1461, by Pope Pius II. In 1970, Pope Paul VI declared her a Doctor of the Church. She and St. Teresa of Avila were the first women to be recognized with this honor.

SAINT PADRE PIO was born at Pietrelcina in the Province of Benevento, in Italy, on May 25, 1887. The second son of a farmer and a housewife, he was baptized the following day in the Church of St. Mary of the Angels in Pietrelcina with the name Francesco, "Francis."

At the age of sixteen, he moved to the Capuchin Priory at Morcone; two weeks later he was clothed in the Franciscan habit and took the name Fra Pio, "Brother Pius." He was ordained a deacon six years later, and a priest the following year. In 1916, he moved to the Priory of San Giovanni Rotondo near Gargano, where he remained for the rest of his life.

In 1918, St. Padre Pio received the gift of stigmata. He tried to hide these marks on his body, but often was unsuccessful. He became famous and sought-after for his mystical teaching and spiritual companionship.

Pope John Paul II beatified St. Padre Pio in 1999. He was then canonized by Pope John Paul II in St. Peter's Square on June 16, 2002.

59

"Serene in our faith and tranquil in our soul, let us pray and continue to pray, because intense and fervent prayer pierces the heavens and is backed up by a divine guarantee."

60

"Pray, pray to the Lord with me, because the whole world needs prayer. And every day, when your heart especially feels the loneliness of life, pray. Pray to the Lord, because even God needs our prayers."

Saint Padre Pio

58

"Never fall back on yourself alone, but place all your trust in God and don't be too eager to be set free from your present state. Let the Holy Spirit act within you. Give yourself up to all His transports and have no fear. He is so wise and gentle and discreet that He never brings about anything but good. How good this Holy Spirit, this Comforter, is to all, but how supremely good He is to those who seek Him."

Set the World on Fire

55

"Live in such a way that your Heavenly Father may be proud of you, as he is proud of so many other chosen souls."

56

"We should remember that the Heart of Jesus has called us not only for our own sanctification, but also for that of other souls. He wants to be helped in the salvation of souls."

57

"I know that your spirit is always wrapped in the darkness of trials, but it is enough for you to know that Jesus is with you and in you."

Saint Padre Pio

52

"In darkness, at times of tribulation and distress of the spirit, Jesus is with you. In such a state, you see nothing but darkness, but I can assure you on God's behalf that the light of the Lord is all around you and pervades your spirit."

53

"You see yourself forsaken and I assure you that Jesus is holding you tighter than ever to His divine Heart."

54

"Jesus, our dear Mother, my little angel, St. Joseph, and our father, St. Francis, are almost always with me."

Set the World on Fire

49

"The Mother of Sorrows is my confidante, my teacher, counselor, and powerful advocate."

50

"Glance at the Divine Master who prayed in the Garden and discover the true ladder that unites earth to Heaven. Discover that humility, contrition, and prayer make the distance between man and God disappear."

51

"Jesus permits the spiritual combat as a purification, not as a punishment. The trial is not unto death but unto salvation."

Saint Padre Pio

47

"Don't allow any sadness to dwell in your soul, because sadness prevents the Holy Spirit from acting freely."

48

"Lord God of my heart, You alone know and see all my troubles. You alone are aware that all my distress springs from my fear of losing You, of offending You, from my fear of not loving You as much as I should love and desire to love You."

Set the World on Fire

44

"Our Lord sends the crosses; we do not have to invent them."

45

"Charity is the measure by which Our Lord judges all things."

46

"Whenever you are seized by melancholy, let your thoughts dwell on that fateful night on which the Son of God began the work of redemption in the solitude of Gethsemane and offer your own sufferings to the Divine Father, along with the sufferings of Jesus."

Saint Padre Pio

41

"Jesus will assist you and give you the grace to live a heavenly life, and nothing whatever will be able to separate you from His love."

42

"Stay with me, Lord, for as poor as my soul is I want it to be a place of consolation for You."

43

"Love Jesus, love Him very much—but to do this, be ready to love sacrifice more."

Set the World on Fire

39

"Oh, for charity's sake, do not deny
me Your help, do not deny me Your
teaching, knowing that the devil
continues more than ever to act with
ferocity against the little boat of
my poor spirit."

40

"Remember that God is within us when
we are in a state of grace and outside of
us when we are in a state of sin. But His
angel never abandons us."

Saint Padre Pio

36

"I fight alone, day and night, against such a strong and powerful enemy.
Who will win?"

37

"Against such an enemy it seems that I will be the one who is vanquished. But what am I saying! Is it possible that the Lord will permit it? Never! I feel, in the deepest part of my spirit, a giant rising to its feet."

38

"May the Most High God always be blessed, Who has never completely abandoned me into the hands of the powers of darkness!"

Set the World on Fire

33

"How is it, O Father, that when I am with
Jesus, all that I have the intention and
resolute will to ask Him never
comes to mind?"

34

"Satan is a powerful enemy."

35

"The devil continually makes a deafening
noise and roars around my poor will. In
this state I can do nothing other than say
with firm resolution, without resentment,
'Long live, Jesus! I believe!'"

Saint Padre Pio

30

"I feel a great love of good reading, but I
read little because my ill-health prevents
me, and because upon opening a book
I become so profoundly recollected that
reading becomes prayer."·

31

"My supreme Good, where are You?
I no longer seem to know You,
I cannot find You. But I am compelled
to seek You. You are the spark
in my dying soul. O God, My God."

32

"How can I repay all that has been done
for me? The answer is to repay all with
prayer to the Lord."

Set the World on Fire

27

"Stay with me, Lord, for You are my life,
and without You, I am without fervor.
Stay with me, Lord, for You are my light,
and without You, I am in darkness."

28

"Stay with me, Lord, to show me Your
will. Stay with me, Lord, so that I hear
Your voice and follow You."

29

"This is a testing ground and the prize
will be awarded up above. We are now in
a land of exile, while our true homeland
is Heaven—to it we must
continually aspire."

Saint Padre Pio

25

"The Lord is a Father, the most tender and best of fathers. He cannot fail to be moved when His children appeal to Him."

26

"Don't worry about the darkness, however much it afflicts you. It is useful, however, to make the Sign of the Cross every now and then on your forehead while saying, 'May the Holy Spirit enlighten our senses and our hearts with his grace,' or 'Seat of Wisdom, pray for us.' In temptations against faith, invoke St. Michael and Sts. Peter and Paul."

Set the World on Fire

23

"Go to the Madonna. Love her! Always say the Rosary. Say it well. Say it as often as you can! Be souls of prayer. Never tire of praying, it is what is essential. Prayer shakes the Heart of God, it obtains necessary graces!"

24

"God commands us to love Him, not as much as He deserves, because He knows our capabilities and therefore He does not ask us to do what we cannot do. But He asks us to love Him according to our strength, with all our soul, all our mind, and all our heart."

Saint Padre Pio

21

"When you feel despised, imitate the kingfisher, who builds its nest on the masts of ships. That is to say, raise yourself above the earth, elevate yourselves with your mind and heart to God, who is the only one who can console you and give you strength to withstand the trial in a holy way."

22

"Be certain that the more the attacks of the devil increase, that much closer is God to your soul."

Set the World on Fire

20

"If you can talk with the Lord in prayer,
talk to Him, offer Him your praise.
If, due to great weariness, you cannot
speak, do not find displeasure in the
ways of the Lord. Stay in the room like
servants of the court, and make a gesture
of reverence. He will see you, and your
presence will be pleasing to Him. He will
bless your silence and at another time
you will find consolation when He takes
you by the hand."

Saint Padre Pio

18

"Stay with me, Lord, for it is necessary to
have You present so that I do not forget
You. You know how easily
I abandon You."

19

"Stay with me, Lord, because I am weak
and I need Your strength,
that I may not fall so often."

Set the World on Fire

16

"You should humble yourself before God
rather than be distressed if he reserves
for you the sufferings of his Son, and
makes you experience your weakness.
You should offer to Him the prayer of
resignation and hope, even when you
fall through frailty, and thank Him for all
the benefits with which He continually
enriches you."

17

"A good heart is always strong, it suffers,
but with tears it is consoled by sacrificing
itself for its neighbor and for God."

Saint Padre Pio

14

"You must remember that you have in Heaven, not only a Father but also a Mother. . . . Let us then have recourse to Mary. She is all sweetness, mercy, goodness and love for us because she is our Mother."

15

"The best means of guarding yourself against temptation are these: watch your senses to save them from dangerous temptation, avoid vanity, do not let your heart become exalted, convince yourself of the evil of complacency, flee away from hate, pray whenever possible. If the soul would know the merit which one acquires in temptations suffered in patience and conquered, it would be tempted to say: Lord, send me temptations."

Set the World on Fire

11

"Kneel down and render tribute and devotion to Jesus in the Blessed Sacrament. Confide all your needs to him. Speak to him with filial abandonment. Give free rein to your heart; and give him complete freedom to work in you as he thinks best."

12

"God enriches the soul which empties itself of everything."

13

"When you are exposed to any trial, be it physical or moral, bodily, or spiritual, the best remedy is the thought of Him who is our life, and not think of the one without joining to it the thought of the other."

Saint Padre Pio

8

"Have patience and persevere in the holy
exercise of meditation. Be content to
begin with small steps till you have legs
to run, better still wings to fly."

9

"The field of battle between God
and Satan is the human soul.
It is in the soul that the battle rages
every moment of life."

10

"Come down to me, Father, into the
secret parts of my soul, full of so much
imperfection and misery. I am not able to
reveal them, but they are numberless."

Set the World on Fire

5

"We have close to us an angelic spirit who never leaves us for an instant from the cradle to the grave, who guides and protects us like a friend or a brother."

6

"You must have boundless faith in the divine goodness, for the victory is absolutely certain."

7

"You say you are anxious about the future, but don't you know that the Lord is with you always and that our enemy has no power over one who has resolved to belong entirely to Jesus?"

Saint Padre Pio

3

"The surest test of love consists in suffering for the loved one, and if God suffered so much for love, the pain we suffer for Him becomes as lovable as love itself."

4

"He wants you entirely for Himself, He wants you to place all your trust and all your affection in Him alone, and it is precisely for this reason that He sends you this spiritual aridity, to unite you more closely to Him."

Set the World on Fire

1

"Have courage and do not fear the assaults of the devil. Remember this forever: it is a healthy sign if the devil shouts and roars around your conscience, since this shows that he is not inside your will."

2

"Prayer is the best weapon we have. It is the key to God's heart. You must speak to Jesus not only with your lips, but with your heart. In fact, on certain occasions you should only speak to Him with your heart."

Saint Padre Pio

SAINT
PADRE PIO

SAINT PADRE PIO

Also available from Paraclete Press...

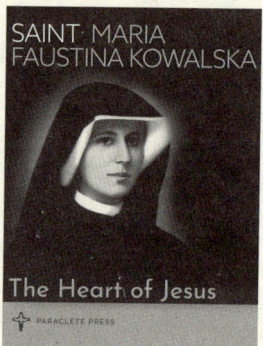

ISBN 978-1-64060-226-7 | $4.99

Available at bookstores
Paraclete Press | 1-800-451-5006
www.paracletepress.com

Set the World on Fire

SAINT CATHERINE OF SIENA

&

SAINT PADRE PIO

PARACLETE PRESS
BREWSTER, MASSACHUSETTS